LEARN SCIENCE WITH MO

STATES OF MATTER

Paul Mason

Michael Buxton

Enslow PUBLISHING

Published in 2026 by Enslow Publishing, LLC
2544 Clinton Street
Buffalo, NY 14224

First published in Great Britain in 2024 by Wayland

Editor: John Hort
Design: Collaborate
Illustrations: Michael Buxton
Science consultant: Peter Riley

Manufactured in the United States of America

CPSIA compliance information: Batch #CSENS26: For further information contact Enslow Publishing LLC, New York, New York at 1-800-398-2504.

Please visit our website, www.enslowpublishing.com. For a free color catalog of all our high-quality books, call toll free 1-800-398-2504 or fax 1-877-980-4454.

Cataloging-in-Publication Data
Names: Mason, Paul. | Buxton, Michael, illustrator.
Title: States of matter / Paul Mason ; illustrated by Michael Buxton.
Description: Buffalo, NY : Enslow Publishing, 2026. | Series: Learn science with Mo | Includes glossary and index.
Identifiers: ISBN 9781978544819 (pbk.) | ISBN 9781978544826 (library bound) | ISBN 9781978544833 (ebook)
Subjects: LCSH: Matter--Properties--Juvenile literature. | Matter--Juvenile literature
Classification: LCC QC173.36 M376 2026 | DDC 530.4--dc23

Contents

The words in **bold** are in the glossary on page 30.

Mo gets WET FEET

Mo and Rory are walking to school. They are talking about Mo's birthday party this weekend.

Mo does not notice the **frozen** puddle up ahead. He slides on the ice and nearly falls over.

The water in the puddles has frozen **solid** during the night. The puddles have turned into mini ice rinks. They are perfect for sliding!

Mo spots an extra big ice patch. The chance for a super slide is too good to miss, but ...

In the middle of the big puddle, the ice is not very thick. As the sun comes up, it gets even thinner as the solid ice turns back into **liquid** water.

For the rest of the morning, Mo leaves wet footprints behind. But they soon disappear in the warm school.

Mo, to avoid getting wet feet again, you need to find out about something called matter.

Matter is what things are made of. We're going to explore three kinds: solids, liquids, and another kind of matter, **gases**. We will look for them at a VERY special occasion ... your birthday party!

Solid, liquid, OR GAS?

Before we get started, there are a few things you need to know about solids, liquids, and gases, Mo.

They each contain tiny building blocks called **particles.** Whether matter is solid, liquid, or gas depends on how closely packed the particles are.

SOLIDS

In solids the particles are tightly packed and cannot move around. They are like you, Rory, Lily, Amy, and Sid all squeezed onto the same couch.

LIQUIDS

In liquids, the particles are less tightly packed. Imagine if Rory, Lily, and Sid got up. There would be lots of space for you and Amy.

GASES

In gases there can be big distances between particles.
Gases are like the playground at playtime, with everyone running around.

DIFFERENT KINDS OF MATTER

SOLID

The particles in a solid stay in the same place all the time.

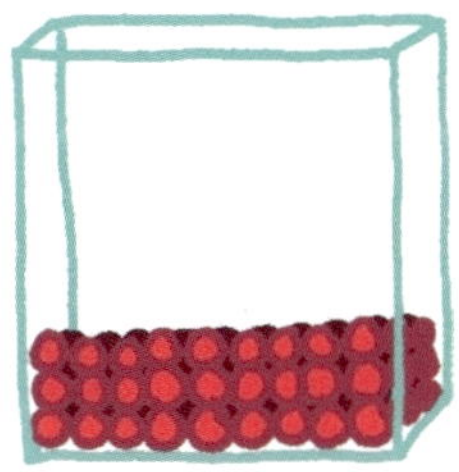

LIQUID

The particles in a liquid can move about, rolling over each other like marbles being tipped about in a jar.

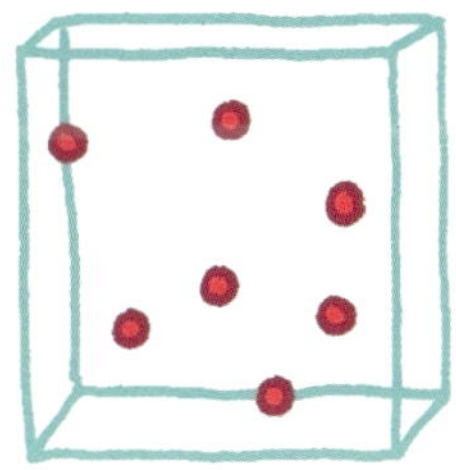

GAS

The particles in a gas can move around and fill their space.

Different kinds of matter behave differently. Which kinds of matter are these, Mo? The answers are on page 32.

Material PROPERTIES

Mo has already planned his birthday party by drawing out all the things that will be there.

Mo, everything in your drawing is made of some sort of matter. Can you work out what kinds of matter they are? Label them solid, liquid, or gas.

Good job, Mo. Those are all correct!

The same kinds of material do not always have the same **properties.** For example, some solids are **flexible,** while others are stiff. Some liquids are **transparent** while others are **opaque.**

A material's properties affect what it is useful for:

Could you make a glass out of wrapping paper?

Could you wrap presents in wood?

Would a balloon be a good water holder?

Good answers, Mo, but Lily might disagree about this last one!

Gas-filled BALLOONS

Mo and Amy are helping to get the party ready. They are decorating the room.

The first job is to blow up some balloons. Mo, what kind of matter would be perfect for filling the balloons?

Air is made of gases, yes. And gas is what you need here. The particles in gas like PLENTY of space to move about. They spread out to fill whatever container they are inside.

If you only add a little gas, it has plenty of space and does not spread out very much.

As more gas is added, it starts to push the balloon outward. The gas wants more room to spread out!

Adding too much gas strains the rubber balloon too far. It pops and the gas escapes.

Mo, let's do a quick quiz to check what you know about gases. Check your answers on page 32.

1. Do the particles in gases:

a) stay still, or

b) move around?

2. Is gas:

a) always the same size, or

b) as big as the container it is inside?

Liquid BEHAVIOR

The monsters are making drinks for the party. They need to work out how many jugs they need.

How many of your friends are coming, Mo?

Like gases, liquids change shape. Unlike gases, liquids stay the same size whatever container they are in. Mo, you can use this fact to check how many jugs of water you need:

One cup ...

The water hits the hard jug. It bounces and splashes about, then settles at the bottom.

Two ...

The second cupful still splashes, but less than when it hit the hard jug.

Three ...

Now there is almost no splash as the water pours in.

Four.

The jug holds four cups of water.

LIQUIDS vs. SOLIDS

When a liquid hits a solid, the solid's particles stay right where they are. The liquid's particles bounce off and make big splashes.

When liquids hit another liquid (for example, water pouring into a bath full of water), the particles move aside to make room for their friends. There is less splash.

Mo, how many jugs do you need for the party?

2 x 4 = 8

ABSORBENT Materials

Dizzy decides to add ice cubes to the orange juice, but things go wrong when Dozy bangs into the table ...

The orange juice and ice cubes go everywhere. They pour off the table, onto the floor and, worst of all, onto Mo's shirt.

No need to worry, Mo, it can go in the washing machine. You need to clean up the mess, though! To mop up the liquid, you need a material that will soak up the liquid. Materials that can do this are called **absorbent.**

Can you say which of these materials are absorbent, Mo?

Paper Towels

Tin foil

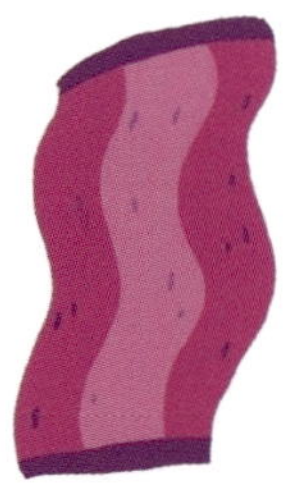
Towel

Plate

Shirt

Great answers, 100% correct! Your reward is to help Dizzy and Dozy mop up.

The ice cubes have warmed up and turned into water. Like water, other materials sometimes change because the temperature has changed. Find out more about this on the next page.

Melting POINT

Lily has volunteered to help decorate the cake. This is risky because Lily really likes chocolate and a lot of it might end up in her belly!

First, Mo's mom heats some water in a pan until it boils. She checks the water is hot enough using a **thermometer.**

Thermometers measure temperature, or how hot or cold something is.

Next, Mom puts a bowl on top of the pan and adds solid chocolate, cream, light molasses, caster sugar, and butter.

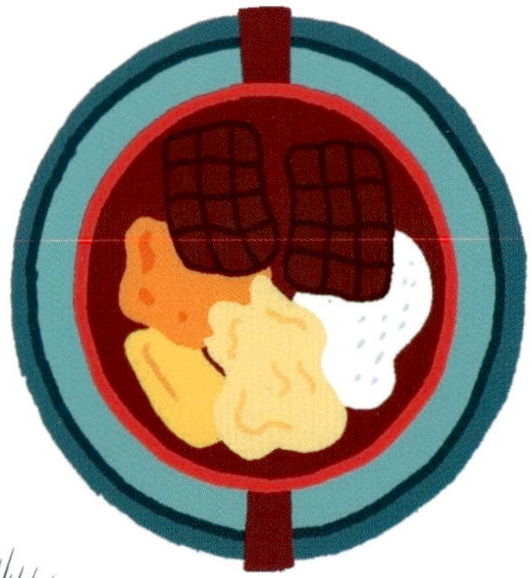

As Mom stirs, the ingredients start to melt. The butter melts first, then the chocolate, and sugar.

Lily takes the bowl and pours the liquid mixture over the cake. Then it goes in the fridge to cool down for later.

Lily, why are you putting the hot sauce in the cold fridge?

So that it gets hard.

Like the butter, chocolate, and sugar, solids melt at different temperatures. This temperature is called their **melting point.**

QUICK QUIZ

Can you put these materials in order of which would melt soonest, as the temperature increased?

 **rock** →  **lava**

 **ice** →  **water**

 **bicycle frame** → 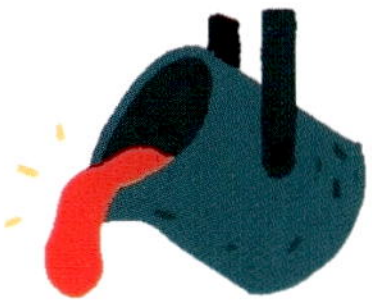 **molton metal**

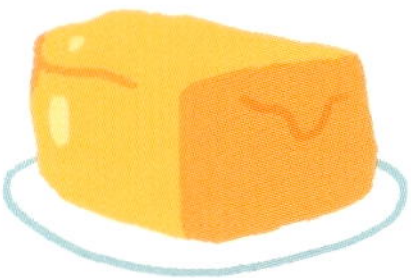 **butter** →  **liquid butter**

Check if you were right on page 32.

DRYING OUT

Mo's favorite Hawaiian party shirt is now all stiff with dried-up orange juice, and the party starts in 90 minutes!

Mo's mom puts the shirt in the washing machine. It takes one hour and the shirt comes out wet. How can you get it dry in time for the party, Mo?

Don't give up. Remember the wet footprints you left at school last week. What made them dry out?

Correct. Heat dried the footprints because of something called **evaporation.**

Evaporation is when particles from a liquid (slowly) turn into a gas and escape into the air. Heat makes this happen faster.

Evaporation is different from boiling. Boiling liquids reach higher temperatures and have bubbles. They turn into gas much more quickly.

QUICK QUIZ

Mo, let's check some facts about evaporation:

1 What happens to liquids when they evaporate?

a) they heat up

b) they turn into a gas

c) both of those

2 Are evaporation and boiling:

a) the same

b) different

c) different but with the same effect?

PRESENT MATERIALS

Mo's friends arrive, bringing with them some excellent presents.

Mo loves playing jokes on people ... and lots of the birthday presents are going to be great fun for this.

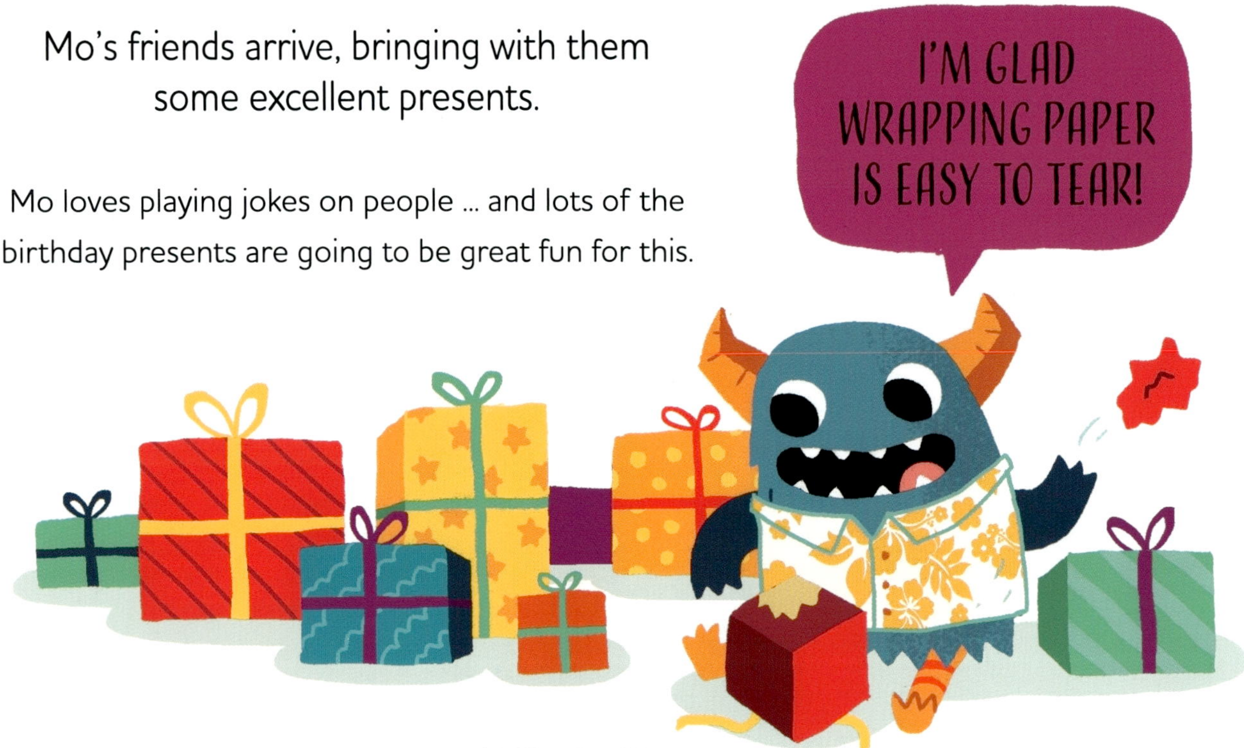

JOKE SWORD

Mo's new sword turns out to be great for fights between friendly knights.

WHOOPEE CUSHION

The whoopee cushion causes Amy an embarrassing moment.

PLASTIC DOG POOP

Mo's dog poop present surprises Mom.

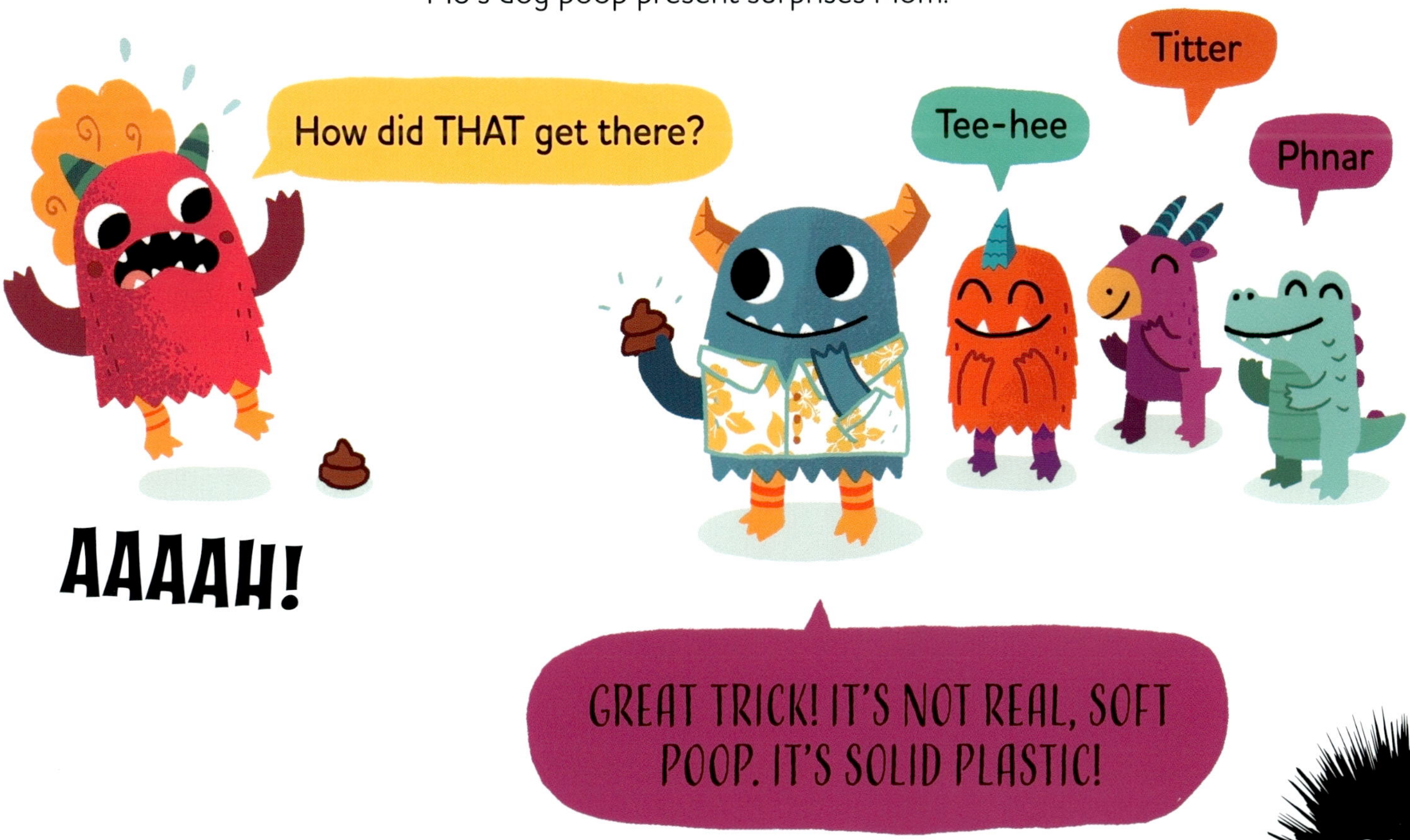

Dozy's Liquid-to-solid FOOTPRINTS

One of Mo's presents was a basketball and hoop. Everyone goes outside to try them out.

First, Mo pumps up the ball, filling it with enough air to feel hard.

1) The ball is pushed downward

2) As it hits the ground, it squishes into a different shape

3) The air inside the ball does not like being squished! It pushes back and the ball bounces up.

Mo, what properties does the basketball's material need to have?

UM, LET'S SEE...
IT NEEDS TO BE BENDY, TO CHANGE SHAPE. AND TOUGH, TO BOUNCE AGAIN AND AGAIN.

Dozy gets a bit overexcited and throws the ball the wrong way. It bounces next door ... and onto some freshly poured concrete! Dozy runs to get the ball and leaves behind crocodile prints. Oops!

A little bit later it starts to rain. Everyone rushes back inside, but Dizzy and Dozy try to get in at the same time. They get stuck in the door.

Unlike liquid concrete, solid doorways don't change shape for monsters!

Chili MIXING

Mo's mom has made chili for the party. Mo, would it surprise you to think that the chili is a good way to learn about how materials mix together?

OK, let's find out a bit more. There are lots of different extra ingredients on the table, which can be mixed into the chili. There are ...

... chili flakes for monsters who like spicy food ...

... yogurt for monsters who find out their chili is TOO spicy ...

... and fresh herbs for monsters who want to add some extra taste.

Materials mix together in different ways. Sometimes they mix together, but stay the same as before. Later you can separate them out again. Sometimes materials combine to make something new. When this happens, you cannot undo it. The old materials disappear.

Mo, can you work out which of the extra ingredients will disappear when they are stirred into the chili?

Great answers, Mo!

What do you think happened to the yogurt?
(Find out if you were right on page 32.)

Trouble with MELTING

The one ingredient EVERYONE adds to their chilli is cheese.

The cheese has been grated into small pieces. It starts off solid. When it hits the hot chilli, though, the cheese changes.

The monsters put big piles of cheese on top of their bowls of chilli. Then they try to eat their way through it. Every spoonful has a great string of cheese dangling from it!

The cheese changes because of heat. At room temperature, it is solid. At about 150 °F (66 °C), though, cheese starts to become liquid.

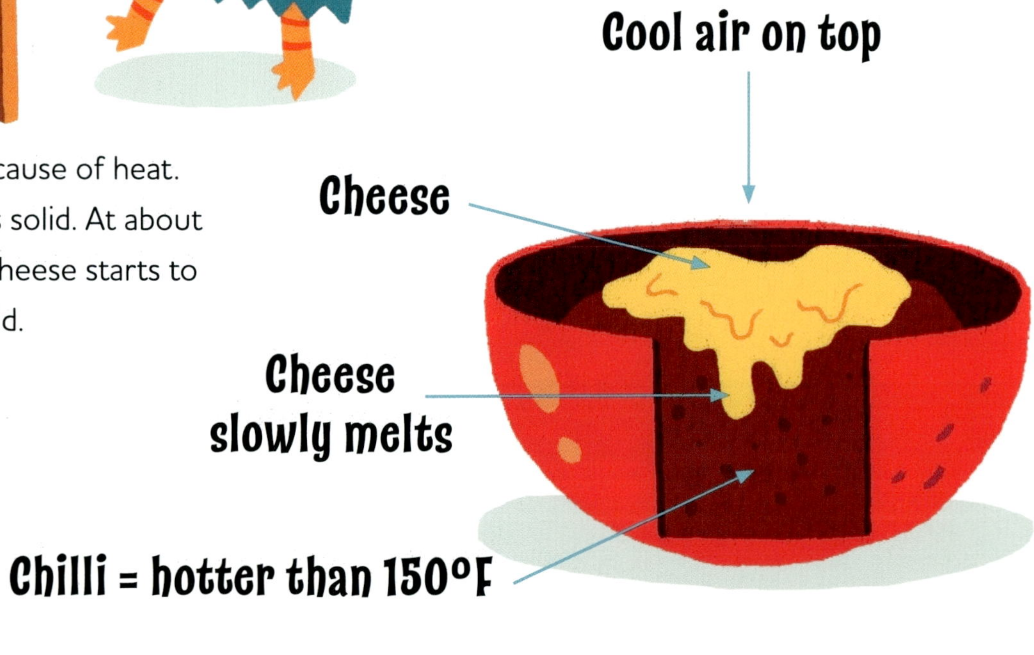

As Mo lifts up a spoonful of chili, the thin string of melted cheese cools down. It starts to go hard again.

QUICK TEMPERATURE QUIZ

Let's just check what Mo found out about materials and temperature.

1) What causes a material to turn from solid to liquid?

2) What is the name for the temperature at which this happens?

Check if you were correct on page 32.

Condensation AND CAKE

The hot chili was steaming when it came in, but so were Mo and the other party guests. How did THAT happen?

In the warm air, the rainwater becomes a gas, or evaporates.
The steam coming off the friends is a gas called **water vapor.**

The room is warm, but the windows are cold. When water vapor touches them it cools down. It turns back into water droplets called **condensation** and the windows go all misty.

The cloudy glass gives everyone a chance to write Mo birthday messages!

Finally the cake arrives. Mo takes a deep breath ... and blows out all the candles at once.

Make a wish, Mo.

Glossary

absorbent
able to take in liquid, for example a towel soaking up water

condensation
the process of water vapor turning into liquid

evaporation
change from a liquid to a gas

flexible
able to bend without breaking

frozen
turned into ice because of getting colder

gas
a kind of matter that is invisible and can move around and spread out to fill its spaces

liquid
kind of matter that can change its shape but not its size

melting point
temperature that causes a solid material to turn into a liquid. Each material has its own melting point, they are not all the same.

opaque
impossible to see through

particles
tiny building blocks of which all materials are made

properties
a quality that something is known by

solid
material that naturally stays the same shape and size

thermometer
device for measuring temperature (how hot or cold something is)

transparent
see-through

vibrate
the back and forth movement of particles in an object

water vapor
water in the form of gas

Books to read

Quick Fix Science: Materials by Paul Mason (Wayland, 2021) Meet Snappy, a young Nile crocodile. Snappy is really interested in science, but not all that good at it yet. In this book, Snappy finds out about materials, what they are and how they change.

See Science: States of Matter by Izzi Howell (Wayland, 2022)
Explore scenes from everyday life that reveal the states of matter all around you, what they are, how they change and explore the water cycle.

Outdoor Science: Materials by Izzi Howell (Wayland, 2022)
Part of a great series that helps children learn about science outdoors. This book is filled with great experiments and activities to do with materials.

Places to visit

Exploratorium
Pier 15, San Francisco, CA, 94111

The museum has displays showing many different kinds of science in action! Learn about different materials, solids, liquids, and gases through hands on exhibits and at-home projects.

The Strong National Museum of Play
One Manhattan Square, Rochester, New York, 14607

This is a fantastic museum aimed completely at young visitors. You can do your own experiments, play educational games, and learn more about different kinds of science

Answers

Page 7

The foot is a solid.

The air inside the football is a gas.

The drink is a liquid.

Page 11

The answer to both questions is b).

Page 17

The order is butter, ice, bicycle frame, and rock.

Page 19

The answer to both questions is c).

Page 25

The yogurt and chili sauce mixed together and became a new one.

Page 27

1) Materials turn from solid to liquid because of heat.

2) The name for the temperature when this happens is 'melting point'.